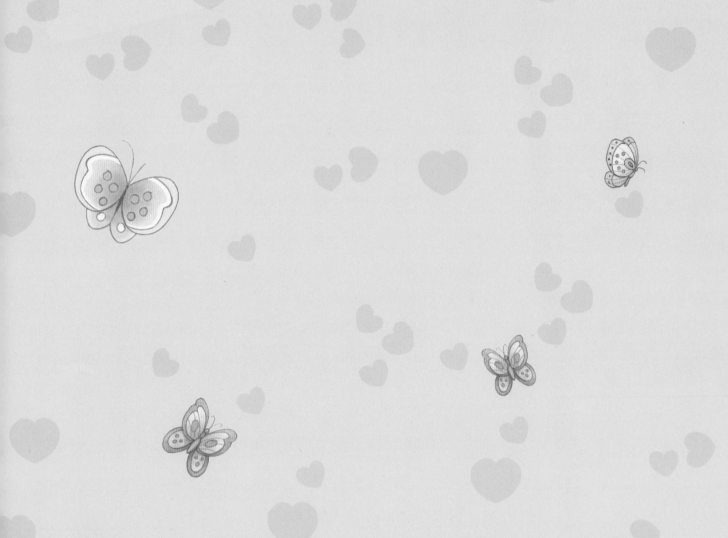

Precious Moments Gift Treasury

Illustrated by Samuel J. Butcher

A GOLDEN BOOK • NEW YORK

© 2004 by Precious Moments, Inc. All rights reserved under International and Pan-American Copyright Conventions. Published in the United States by Golden Books, an imprint of Random House Children's Books, a division of Random House, Inc., New York, and simultaneously in Canada by Random House of Canada Limited, Toronto. Golden Books, A Golden Book, and the G colophon are registered trademarks of Random House, Inc.

The material contained in this book was taken from the following Golden Books publications:
What A Wonderful World © 1992 by Precious Moments, Inc. • *Little Thank-You's* © 1997 by Precious Moments, Inc.
Little Prayers © 1997 by Precious Moments, Inc. • *Happiness Is . . .* © 1995 by Precious Moments, Inc.
A Child Is . . . © 1995 by Precious Moments, Inc. • *A Friend Is . . .* © 1992 by Precious Moments, Inc.
Love Is . . . © 1990 by Precious Moments, Inc. • *A Wedding Is Beautiful* © 1998 by Precious Moments, Inc.
Let's Be Thankful © 1998 by Precious Moments, Inc. • *Little Blessings* © 1996 by Precious Moments, Inc.
Heaven's Little Helpers ©1995 by Precious Moments, Inc.

Precious Moments is a registered trademark of Precious Moments, Inc. Licensee Random House, Inc. All rights reserved.
ISBN: 0-375-83130-4

www.goldenbooks.com
MANUFACTURED IN CHINA
10 9 8 7 6 5 4 3 2 1

Contents

What A Wonderful World

God gave this world to you and me.

It's priceless, yet it's also free.

It's beautiful beyond compare,

and He has left it in our care.

Every day begins anew,

like a rose sparkling with the dew.

They blossom in the morning sun

and bloom until the day is done.

A little seed becomes a tree

and gives its shade to you and me.

Every creature,
great and small,

the Lord above has made them all.

The bear, the bee, the kangaroo

all share this world with me and you.

High above us in the sky,

we watch the silver
clouds go by.

They bring the gentle rain our way,

and rainbows brighten up our day.

And as we watch the setting sun,

another perfect day is done.

God gave this world to you and me.

He lit the stars above.

By seeing all the things He made . . .

we know that God is love.

Little Thank-You's

Thanks for sun, for wind and snow,
for rain that makes the flowers grow.

And thanks for friends to share each day
Sunny, soggy, bright, or gray.

Thanks for cats and thanks for dogs,
for singing birds and leaping frogs.

Thanks for bunnies, bears, and doves,
for all our friends and all our loves.

Thanks for pears and apples,
for daisies in their rows.

for pumpkins and pine trees,
for everything that grows.

Thanks for the drum with its rum-pum-pum
And the bell with its ringy-ding.

Thanks for the flute with its tootly-toot.
They make me want to sing.

Thanks for games and goodies
At picnics in the park.

Thanks for funny stories
Round a campfire when it's dark.

Thanks for ice cream when it's hot,
And soup on a winter's day.

I hope the calf's as happy
With its meal of munchy hay.

Thank you, God,
for a happy day.

Give me a happy tomorrow,
I pray.

I wonder what I'll dream tonight,
Here in my cozy bed.

Perhaps I'll dream of kings and queens,
Or just of my old bear, Ted.

My guardian angel
spends the night.

And keeps me safe
Till morning's light.

Thanks for the sun . . . thanks for the moon . . .
Thanks for the stars so bright.

Thanks for watching over me—
Morning, noon and night.

Thank you, God,
for books and toys

To share with other
Girls and boys.

Thank you, God, for the earth and sky,
for oceans deep and mountains high,

For summer, winter, fall, and spring
Thank you, God, for everything.

Happiness Is . . .

Happiness is taking a bubble bath . . .

or sharing an ice cream soda with a friend.

Happiness is blowing out the candles on your birthday cake . . .

and receiving a special gift.

Happiness is riding a scooter with your friends . . .

or playing dress-up.

Happiness is singing your favorite song . . .

or playing a big, round drum.

But most of all, happiness is . . .

being with people you love.

A Child Is...

A child is kind . . .

to all creatures great and small.

A child is curious . . .

and likes to explore.

A child loves to snuggle . . .

and share ice cream with a special friend.

A child is a little helper . . .

who's glad to lend a hand.

But most of all,
a child is an angel . . .

a special gift from God.

A Friend Is...

A friend is . . .

someone to pick flowers with.

A friend is someone to play with . . .

or sing with.

With a friend
you can take a walk

or go for a ride!

A friend will write you a letter . . .

or call you on the phone.

But most of all a friend is . . .

someone who will always be there.

Love is helping a plant grow . . .

and running with your puppy.

Love is visiting a sick friend . . .

and wishing another friend
happy birthday.

Love is sharing . . .

and caring.

Love is receiving a present . . .

and giving a present.

Love is playing together . . .

and love goes on forever!

A Wedding Is Beautiful

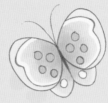

I'm going to be a flower girl,
My sister asked me to!

You see, she's had this boyfriend
for a year now, maybe two.

And he "proposed." That means he asked
To marry her, I guess,

'Cause since then they have been "engaged"—
That means she said *yes!*

They've had to plan their wedding
Down to every last detail,

Like designing invitations—
I helped put them in the mail!

Now the day has come! The church is full!
It's time to start the service!

And I'm the first one down the aisle.
(I'm just a little nervous!)

My little cousin brings the ring
And comes right after me.

The maid of honor follows him
And, oh, so gracefully.

And now here comes the handsome groom;
He winks and makes me smile!

And then—at last—the lovely bride
Comes floating down the aisle.

Then side by side they vow to love
Each other all their life,

And with a kiss become at last
A husband and a wife.

It's time to cut the wedding cake
And let the fun begin!

The newlyweds start dancing first,
And soon we all join in!

The ladies gather round and try
To catch the bride's bouquet.

Thank goodness photos save each moment
Of this precious day.

And once the celebration is over,
Off the lovebirds race.

To spend a happy honeymoon
In some romantic place.

Perhaps when they come back they'll start
Their own new family.

I'll have a niece or a nephew—
Either one is fine with me.

My sister's married! Now I dream
About my wedding day.
I dream about the dress I'll wear
As I toss my own bouquet.

And who will I be marrying?
My head is in a whirl!
This is almost as much fun
As being flower girl!

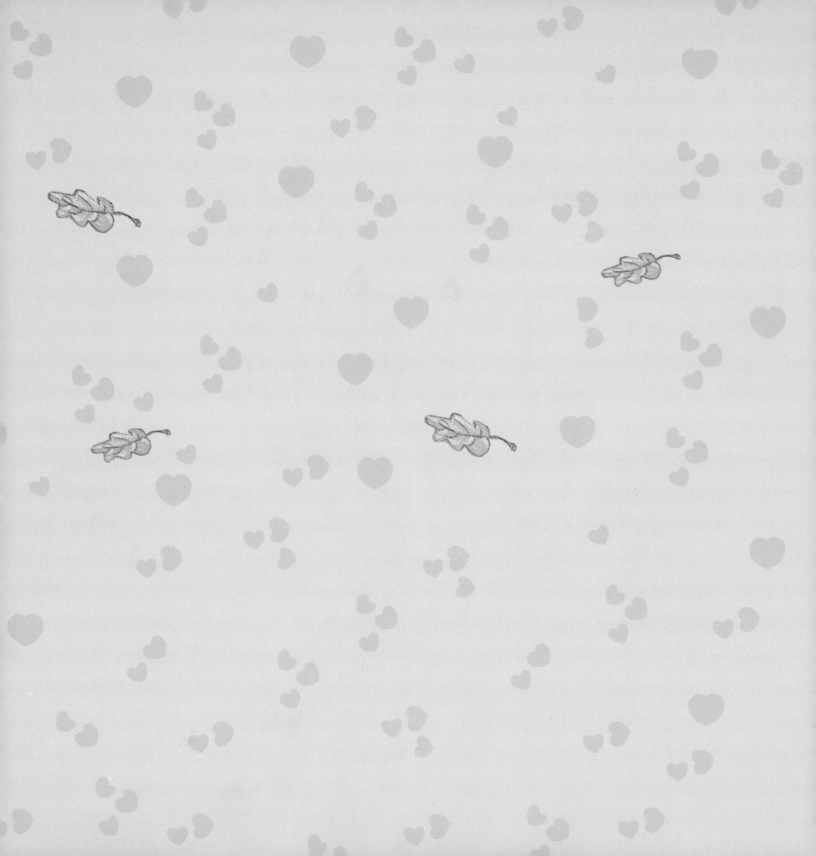

Precious Moments

Let's Be Thankful

Long ago the first Thanksgiving
Dinner was prepared . . .

By neighbors giving thanks to God
for blessings they had shared.

We have Thanksgiving still
As they did centuries before,

Reminding me of all the things
That I am thankful for.

Like Mom and Dad, who love me,
And who always understand . . .

My older brother, who is there
To lend a helping hand . . .

My friends who help me get back up
When my plans don't succeed,

And friends who give a gentle push
When that is all I need.

I'm thankful for my teachers, too,
Who help to stretch my mind.

And open up new worlds to me
With books of every kind.

I'm thankful for the time I have
To play games with my team.

And thankful for the time I have
Alone—to think and dream.

And music—I'm so thankful
for the songs that we can sing . . .

And the music that surrounds us,
Made by every living thing!

I'm thankful for this world which God
Has given to us all,

for the endless wonders in it—
Every creature great and small . . .

The creatures living in the forests,
Jungles, fields, and seas . . .

And animals that live with us
And join our families!

I'm thankful for the gentle breeze
That rustles through my hair,

And soft, cool showers that
feed the flowers
That pop up everywhere!

I'm thankful for the vegetables
And fruits that Nature brings,

With which we make Thanksgiving pies
And other tasty things!

Thanksgiving lets us praise what God
Has given me and you.
And joins us all in peace and love—
I'm thankful for that, too!

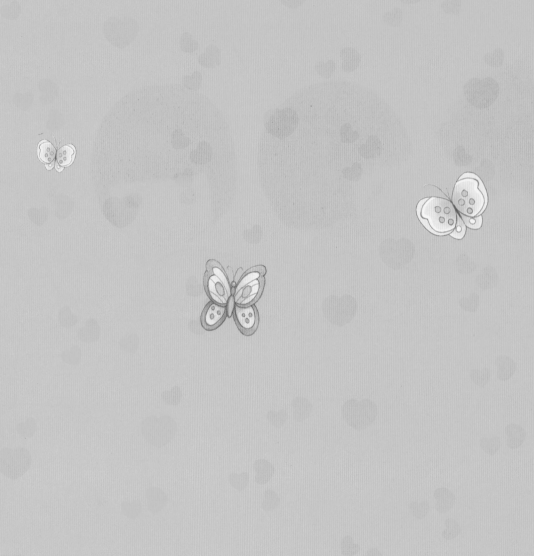

Little Blessings

Babies are a gift from heaven,
Sent to grace our lives.

Each one's a little blessing—
from the moment it arrives!

They start to grow the day they're born—
And some can get quite tall!

While some are happy, year to year,
To just stay rather small!

They come in different colors
And wear coats of many types.

Some have hair and some are bare
And some have spots or stripes!

At first they can't care for themselves
And need some help from others—

A mother or a father or
Big sisters and big brothers!

All little blessings need a home—
A place in which to dwell—

That protects them and keeps them safe,
Like a turtle in its shell!

Every little blessing needs
Some healthy food to eat—

Though most prefer the taste
   of something
Rich and, oh, so sweet!

They're frisky and they're full of fun
And love to romp and play,

So little blessings also need
A lot of rest each day!

Some don't like the water much,
While others soak for hours!

Some just love to play outdoors
Beneath the cool rain showers!

If they try too much too soon,
They'll often take a fall.

Before they run and jump and play,
Most must learn to crawl.

As little blessings grow and learn,
They need a helping hand

And hugs to give them confidence
from friends who understand!

At times they may feel happy
And at times they'll shed a tear.

But most of all they love to share
Good times with someone dear!

Each little blessing's different
In a million special ways,
But all of them bring love and joy
To brighten up our days!

Heaven's Little Helpers

Heaven's angels watch our world
Although we're not aware.

Like shepherds guarding little lambs,
They tend to us with care.

From the moment we are born
They're with us every day,

Sitting close beside us
As we learn to crawl and play!

We grow up very quickly
And they're with us as we do.

And every birthday that we have,
They celebrate it, too!

Whenever we try something new
An angel's by our side.

And every time that we succeed
All heaven beams with pride!

They help to keep us on our feet
Whenever we might stumble

And help us get back up again
If we should take a tumble!

The angels light the way for us
When we are feeling lost

And lift us over tricky paths
Too difficult to cross.

When we're sad the angels come
And help us dry a tear.

And when we're hurt they nurse us till
Our pains all disappear!

They watch what time we rise each day
And when we go to bed.

And as we fall asleep they light
The bright stars overhead.

In the winter angels decorate
Our world with sparkling snow.

And in the spring they send us rain
That makes the flowers grow!

They make bright rainbows in the sky—
Too beautiful for words—

And fill the air around us
With lovely songs of birds!

The angels guard each living thing,
The large as well as small.

And pray for peace and happiness
To touch us, one and all!

Let's give thanks for all the angels
Sent from up above,
Who bring us comfort, give us hope,
And fill our world with love!